Angel Productions presents...

The Angel Rules

1. There is NO SUCH THING as OVER THE TOP!
2. ALWAYS choose your color scheme FIRST!!
3. Know your audience, and KNOW how to work them!!
4. DO NOT Allow other's Idiocracy EFFECT YOU!!!
5. NEVER -EVER leave another Angel hanging.
6. "It is what it is," means "It is what YOU make it."
7. "Don't ask an Angel a question if you don't want the real answer."
8. An Angel cannot be out done.
9. Do Not Call Your Self an Angel when your not.
10. Live the life you are given!

The Little Angel Book for Girls

Wendy Torres

Dedications

To my very own little Angels – Brennan, Zyonne-Elizabeth & Nikka, and all the girls out there search to find your purpose in this world. You were made for greatness so start living.

Acknowledgements

To one of the most supportive hubbies in the World of Angeldom! You are my rock!

T o a mother that pushed me to be everything I could ever think of **and** anyone else that got in the way of that!

To Shauna - Angel 2 & co-author of The Rules. Your mind shall be preserved in the Angel Hall of Fame – FOR LIFE!

To my Family and Friends that have to live with my Angelesque personality

About That...

What's your dream? Cheerleading, Dance, Medical School, Writing, Teaching…Theater… Whatever your dreams are, you are not going to wake up one day and just "be that." You are going to have to work for your dreams, and here is how The Angels do it…..

Table of Content

The Angel Rules

---

1. There Is No Such Thing As *Over The Top*!

2. Always Choose Your Color Scheme *First*!!

3. Know Your Audience, and *Know* How To Work Them!!

4. Do Not Allow Others' *Idiocracy* Affect You!!!

5. NEVER-EVER Leave Another Angel Hanging. This is a Cardinal Sin!

6. *It Is What it is*, means "*It Is What YOU Make It.*"

7. Don't Ask an Angel a Question If You Don't Want The Real Answer.

8. An Angel Cannot Be Out Done.

9. Do Not Call Yourself an Angel When You're Not.

10. Live The Life You Are Given!

What is an Angel?

More like "who" are the Angels. "Angels" define young ladies who have a lot of talent, strength, and direction. Angels know who they are! They are strong and "girly" at the same time. They have a purpose and they can "work it, girl." You show me a gifted, spunky girl who thinks for herself, does her own thing, and is too busy living her own life to be jealous or envious of other girls, and I'll show you a true Angel.

Angels can stand alone, but when you bring them together to complete a task, they can get it done! Angels always bring something to the table. We are task oriented. WE LIKE CHALLENGING THINGS!

Angels are young ladies that embrace the learning process. They know their own strengths and weaknesses, and they know how to work them! Angels make things happen. We have our own vocabulary. We don't try to be somebody else! We are all very different – a key requirement. Angels don't allow others to define them. But we realize we need GREAT people in our lives to help us be our best, so we *choose* each other.

There is one thing we all have in common – *The Angel Rules!* We all live by *The Rules*. We are bound by *The Rules!* By applying *The Rules*, there is no end to the possibilities of living an Angelesque life. If you can embrace The Angel Rules, then you're ready to be the "You" God intended... the Angel Way.

Basic Angel Vocabulary:

Delete- Removing an action when there is an inappropriate response, or something doesn't even deserve the few seconds of time it would take for you to process the hair-brained thought or comment.

Rewind- action used to turn back time; to re-evaluate a situation. It can be used to re-emphasize a point or to "delete" a point-of-action.

Refresh- when a power play you orchestrated has lost its zeal and is in need of refreshing or re-do. This often happens when others around you forget the rules and need a reminder.

"About That" – Our way of saying that we are going to have to go back on a statement an Angel has told you earlier. This happens when one Angel makes a decision about an issue: then after discussing it with other Angels, she realizes that the first decision was not going to work. It's a lot nicer than "Ooo sorry Boo!

"Umm, Imagine That" – When somebody does something or something happens that you said would happen. An Angel never gloats; she just smiles!

"Yeah...uh ...NO!" *(Done with a smile for "yeah" and then a straight face with a hard "NO!")* This is a power move! It's very direct and a little aggressive. So don't use it if you do not want people mad with you.

ANGELDOM – The Kingdom where the principles of the Angels and their Rules reign.

ANGELESQUE - The art of style, method, manner, fashion, approach, and essence of being an Angel. Being Angelesque is the manner in which one conducts business and completes tasks.

Your Name – esque – those things that are uniquely "you." And refers to the way you do those things that set you apart. Example: Writing a poem for my hubby for Valentine's Day is so "Wendy-esque." It's something people expect me to do.

AIT – Angel In Training

"You know that's not going to end well, right?" Angels are bound to tell the truth to those who ask. Sometimes that truth is letting others, even Angels, know the path they are taking is a dead end!

IDIOCRACY - Being governed by a consistent state of idiocy; being fatuitous; foolish decision making.

Rule # 1

There Is No Such Thing As Over The Top!

It's Your Life. Do It Right And Do It BIG!

Angels do think over the top! An Angel allows herself room to visualize the impossible, and then she spends the rest of her life trying to make it happen. The difference between an Angel and a dreamer is that an Angel has the nerve, drive, and initiative to manifest her dreams, or at least she will "live" trying. We move from the position of a day dreamer, wishing and hoping things go well with our lives, to a position of action. Angels look at their dreams, talents, and gifts, then begin to calculate and strategize how to develop the ideas in their heads into actual tangible things. The word *manifest* means to materialize or make tangible that which is intangible such as dreams, thoughts, and ideas into a physical object. If you want to be a doctor, lawyer, nurse, FBI agent, chef, a faithful follower of Christ, a dedicated mother, the next Supreme Court Justice, or whatever your heart yearns for, you will have to work for it. It will not just come to your house, knock on the door, and introduce itself. God lays out a plan for our lives, but we have to pick it up and run with it!

Dreams are made for sharing. An Angel knows she can't do the impossible all by herself! What are your areas of influence? Who do you know that can help you reach your dreams? It's okay to ask for help. All true Angels have a circle of friends that help them fly. Do you really think you could do it alone? You've got to do the big thing. If you can think it – it can be done – with divine help!

Psalms 37:4 reads "Delight thyself also in the LORD; and he shall give thee the desires of thine heart." What does that mean? The biggest adventure of our teen-ages years is beginning the exploration of "OURSELVES;" developing the answer to the question, "Who Am I?" and "What Am I About?" It can be an exciting time in life. Middle and high school bring opportunities for new friends, new ideas, new activities, and new styles. As we seek our purpose in life and begin to define our dreams, there is one sure fire way to get a direct clear understanding of who you are and what you have to offer to the world. A solid connection and relationship with God is win-win in the game of self esteem, self-awareness, confirmation, and

affirmation.   When we look to God for direction
,"Delighting ourselves in Him," we find that He, in
return, gives us our desires.

This means two things: 1) in our time spent with the
LORD, He puts (imparts) ideas, dreams, visions,
talents, and gifts inside us. So let's be very clear: the
great ideas we think up, the careers we dream about, and
the things in our minds that we feel are too big to ever
accomplish, all come from God (if those dreams and
ambitions are moral and ethical that is, lol).

2) After we identify, understand, and connect with
those dreams, He waits to give us the provisions -
(everything we need) to make our "hearts desires" come
true!

The key to "Being All You Can Be" is knowing who you
are!

An Angel knows who she is. Knowing the answer to
this question is key to living a successful life. People
spend so much time searching for "themselves" that
they never live; they just exist.

An Angel also understands "whose" she is and that she
has a purpose that drives her "over imaginative"
personality. My heart goes out to those who don't know
that they have a reason for being - existing!   That is

why it is imperative that Angels *press in* - a pushing, a feverish and intensive search, look for, and find out who we really are. We should celebrate our talents and our gifts. They give us focus. They are the beginning of Purpose.

My Rule 1 Thoughts

_____

_____

_____

_____

_____

_____

_____

_____

_____

_____

_____

_____

_____

_____

_____

_____

_____

_____

_____

_____

_____

What are your talents and gifts?

My skills_____

_____

_____

Things I want to learn_____

_____

_____

My Interests:

1._____

2._____

3._____

4._____

5._____

My Dreams: When I close my eyes I see myself...

_____

_____

_____

_____

_____

_____

What jobs or actions would you complete without pay?

_____

_____

My own Life Rule #1: _____

_____

_____

Phil 4:13 I can do all things through Christ which strengtheneth me

Rule #2

Always Choose Your Color Scheme First.

The Angel Concept which means - PLAN EVERYTHING!

1. All true Angels understand that planning is ALWAYS necessary!

Everybody has dreams. Angels live their lives to make those dreams come true. You can do whatever your mind can think up. It just takes a little planning, constant energy, and a lot of faith.

2. Do your homework.

What will you need to accomplish your dreams? Will you need a specific skill or credentials such as a degree or certification? You can get a degree in just about anything. Doing well in class can add up to scholarship and grant money. Post-secondary school – college, trade schools, and certification programs are definitely needed if you plan on doing more than fast food, retail, or other entry-level positions.

 Almost all professions require some post-high school training. However, everyone is not college bound, and there are many ways to prepare yourself for a great future without a four- year college program.

 You can go to school in specific areas: dance, theater, vocal training, visual arts, and architecture. Also, there are online programs you can complete while at home. Some schools specialize in specific licensing (clerical or electrician) or certificates (nail technician or hair stylist) that take six months to a year to complete. Some programs permit you to work while you learn, or you may be able to find employment with a company that provides on-the-job training and opportunities to advance.. Whatever the plan, you need to begin paving the way to your future by being seriously engaged in your school work and subjects today. The work you do today can help you identify what you want to accomplish tomorrow. This is a key step to start your dream building.

3. Surround yourself with people that believe in you

You are only as great as the company you keep. While you do not need to look to others to affirm "Who" you are, you do need people to support you as you reach for your goals. Be very careful about sharing your dreams. You want those around you to be truthful and faithful. Be leery of people that say everything is great. True friends will tell you when things aren't quite right. See Rule 5. Remember, Angels will help you carry (accomplish) your dreams. It takes a village to raise a child and likewise you will not make it to the finish line of your dreams alone. Haters will do everything to kill them.

4. Put your plans in writing

"Write the Vision," simply means put the ideas in your head down on paper. Think of every detail. What colors and materials are needed? What does your end product look like in your mind? Make a list. Make a schedule; be realistic. "Rome wasn't built in a day." You are mistaken if you think you can play-it-by-ear to become the best "you" possible. If you're serious about it, buy a notebook and write your ideas out. Remember this Angel motto - **Think it; write it, and speak to it – daily!**

5. Count the Cost

What are you willing to give up in order to make your dreams a reality? They will take time away from other things. It may cost money – tutors or piano lessons cost, but remember you want to be the best. Family and friends will have to wait some days. You might have to practice, practice, practice, and YEAH it's gonna hurt. That which doesn't kill us leaves pretty bad bruises...lol! No seriously, nothing worth having comes easy. Your economics textbook calls this Opportunity Cost. *Opportunity cost is the value of the next best choice that one gives up when making a decision.*

The point is everything we do in life comes with a cost. An Angel knows to count them up before she moves forward.

6. Just Do It!

Once you have a plan and a strong core or support group, WORK YOUR PLAN! If you need to improve your skills, **start practicing**. If you need money to get started, **start saving**. If college is the way to go, **pay attention** to your grades and establish good work habits. Take advantage of every opportunity to earn scholarships. If you are rejected after each tryout, audition, or submission, **ask for feedback**. Then use that feedback not to cry over, but to improve. Everyone needs improvement with something.

Once you have an idea, **embrace it**. Do your homework and position yourself to make things happen. While college degrees may not reflect all your abilities or talents, you will need something beyond a high school diploma to demonstrate your seriousness and commitment to your dreams. Write the vision and make it plain -plan it out. Count the cost, and hold on to people who believe in you. These are the foundational ingredients for the great start of a good life, a God ordained life.

My Rule 2 Thoughts

Goals for 20_____

1. _____
2. _____
3. _____

5- Year Goals

_____
_____
_____
_____
_____

What skills will you need?

_____
_____
_____
_____
_____
_____

Money needed_____ Time needed _____

How are you going to acquire them:_____

_____

_____

Are you willing to work for your dreams?

_____

_____

My Own Life Rule #2 _____

_____

Luke 14:28 For which of you, desiring to build a tower, does not first sit down and count the cost, whether he has enough to complete it

Rule #3

Know Your Audience, and *Know* How To Work Them!

An Angel must possess the charisma to make things happen. You have to understand the people around you. School principals are different from friends, and parents of friends are different from your boss. Everyone is looking for something from you. An Angel knows how to be what she needs, while still being herself.

An Angel is always in the middle of the action – **we do not spectate**! "Get it done," "Hustle," "Move it," "By any Means Necessary", these are all phrases you may hear an Angel say. Wherever there are major projects being constructed, you are sure to find an Angel or two in the midst. If your coach wants to see you hustle during practice, you better *get your hustle on* from beginning to end. If you want to be the best, you can't just talk about it; you have to "be" about it.

Don't Get it Twisted.

We spend so much time trying to impress the wrong people. What you wear, what you have, or don't have, are not the attributes that are going to advance your dreams. They may get you a senior superlative award or a photo or two in the year book. But when it's all said and done, your classmates are not your audience. They are trying to find out who they are just like you are!

Know Your Audience

Your "audience "is the group of people that play a part in helping you reach your goals. These are people whose job it is to measure whether your effort is good enough - teachers, coaches, private tutors, interviewers, professional judges, professors, and critics. Respect their words and use their critiques to drive your pursuit for excellence.   There will be some that say "NO," but you have to have confidence in what you are and know that there is a "Yes" out there for you.

Angel Note: Since you know you are going to encounter these people, it does you well to learn what they are looking for ahead of time.

Spend the first six weeks of a class getting to know your teacher. Learn what the teacher requires and produce that. In my college World History class, I learned my professor's terminology, the type of words he used over and over (Like when I say "Angelesque"). During essay exams I always used that same vernacular (words). I made an "A" in all three classes I took under his instruction. What will it take for your parents to trust you? If you really want your curfew extended or that new phone or car, what are you going to do to show them that you are worthy of these new perks? Do you really think that "D" in Biology is going to push your dad to the mall for the new I-phone...Yeah...uh...NO!

Understanding and working your audience is not the same as manipulating people. Manipulation is deceptive. Angels don't lie. We are truthful. Being trustworthy is a really big part of Angel-essence! So, trying to fake out your parents or conjuring up some way to get over on those who are trying to help you is so not Angel-istic! Think about it. After you have schemed, plotted and planned, you could have used all that time and energy to do what you were supposed to do. Take it from one who REALLY KNOWS...just do the right thing! It's less stress!

Those that Spectate

Your haters are **not** your audience. They are your spectators – so smile for the camera! There will always be those who don't want to see you make captain or student body president! It doesn't matter that they can't do the job; their self-hatred won't let them be happy for your success. Don't be angry and go all "Bonquinsha" on them. This will lower your stock! Remember that those who do not understand the rules can't live by them.

Angle Note: Angels know who and whose they are so there is a confidence we have that reassures us that we can survive when our egos are knocked around. **And your ego will get knocked around.** If someone else does not know their purpose, why would you expect them to celebrate your destiny? Think about it. I'm just sayn'; people that don't understand God's plan for their lives cannot help you on your journey.

Be careful not to get side tracked by the trick of the enemy. Distractions come to throw you off. Getting caught up in drama can cause a definite derailment. NO ONE can stop what God has for you BUT YOU. You're HIS little Angel!

My Rule 3 Thoughts

_____

_____

_____

_____

_____

_____

_____

_____

_____

_____

_____

_____

_____

_____

_____

_____

_____

_____

_____

_____

Who is your Audience?

List the (type of) people you will come in contact with to reach your goals from page(s) 6 & 8.

_____

_____

_____

_____

_____

_____

Who makes up your "Amen" corner – those who support your dreams?

1. _____   2. _____

3. _____   4. _____

5. _____   6. _____

Notice to all your haters – complete then declare aloud

"I see you Lookn'

"Got your shades on, watch me

_____ Get some glasses, to see

me _____ Take a seat and

don't miss it when I _____

_____

_____

_____." Repeat as needed!

My Own Life Rule #3_____

_____

_____

Malachi 1:9 And now, I pray you, entreat the favor of God, that he may be gracious unto us:

Rule # 4

Do Not Let Others' Idiocracy Affect You!!!

Your life will be filled with its own trials and tribulations - WHY would you purposely allow others to cause you any extra grief!

While people will always play a huge part in your life, it is very important that you do not get "caught up in them." High School clicks can be so damaging, even into adulthood. How many women live out their adult lives stuck in the categories and labels they were given in middle and high school? Even worse is the damage we do to ourselves in our twenties and thirties because we are trying to prove those labels untrue. It is so important that you understand who you are as a young woman. You cannot allow someone else to define your existence. Only God the Father can tell you who you are.

It is the job of our parents to speak life over us, nurture us, tell us all the visions they saw in our little eyes as infants. God gave them that assignment.

If you have parents, grandparents, loved ones, pastors, or teachers that are telling you the great things they see in you – BELIEVE THEM! Embrace the good, receive the best, ponder the not so good and then use it to improve your character – your attitude, so you can be the best "you" possible.

Think about it, why would you let another teen, girl or boy, who is wondering who they are, tell you who you are or what you are going to be. Don't let someone tell you you're ugly, you're fat, you're dumb, or stupid, and when they do, out of stupidity, do not allow that "death" into your heart. Ask some of your teachers and parents what people said about them when they were young, or to see their ninth grade yearbook photos. A lot changes from 15 to 25. Teen years are only 6 of your whole life.

If you are really trying to make your dreams come true, you don't have time to get caught up in the wrong crowds. Girl clicks, gangs, crime groups, or sex groups – you show me a group of kids that are willing to throw their lives away in promiscuity, drugs, or criminal activity and I'll show you a group of kids that do not know that they are loved! It will be very hard to create your dreams behind bars, high, with a baby, or a STD.

Angel Note: <u>Globally</u> - Every fifteen seconds, another person age 15-24 becomes infected with HIV/AIDS. In the U.S., at least half of all new infections are among people under the age of 25. *1

In the U.S. where a high school education is free, the high school graduation rate only reaches 71 percent. (2009). *2

U.S. students from the 50 largest cities have about a 50/50 chance of earning a basic high school diploma. Specifically, in Atlanta, that number is 46 %. *3 While Birmingham City Schools graduated less than 45% of white or Black students in 2006. *4
I'm not sayn'...I'm just sayn'!

To be strong enough to stand up to the pressure of your peers, you have to really know who you are.

You are the Daughter of the Most High God.

This is a very important title. It makes you royalty. It means, no matter if your earth parents are good or bad, you are connected to the source of all grace, favor, mercy, and love. You have privileges and rights that make you special. You are surrounded by an entourage of angel body guards who protect you from things you are not even aware of. You have access to the best advisor in the Holy Spirit, and you have the greatest big brother – Jesus Christ. When your father blesses you with gifts and talents, all eyes are on you as you walk into the room. When people want to know how you got this or that, just say, "My daddy gave this to me!" Your future is already laid out for you. All you have to do is spend a little time with your Dad to get your instructions on how to get it done. It's all in His Will! Developing a genuine relationship with The LORD qualifies you to an inheritance that you can access TODAY. You don't have to wait for someone to die to get these gifts. As the Daughter of the Most High God, our Father is living and making provisions for us daily. People know who your Family is. They've heard of your brother and know the power your daddy wields, so all you have to do is let it be known that you have the same characteristics as your father. You should look like

Him, act like Him, sound like him, exhibit His mannerisms and character.

If you thought Donald Trump's children or the Hilton sisters had it made because of who their parents are, I dare you to really grab hold to the understanding of who your father is and that He loves you and wants you as His daughter. We all love and admire the daughters of the President of the United States, but even their privilege and position are nothing in comparison to the closeness and position you hold in the heart of God. He loves you and has great gifts for your life .

Embrace who you truly are and live the Angelesque life you were called to Live!

My Rule 4 Thoughts

_____

_____

_____

_____

_____

_____

_____

_____

_____

_____

_____

_____

_____

_____

_____

_____

_____

_____

_____

Who are you?

My beliefs _____
_____
_____
_____

My values_____
_____
_____

Things I care most about_____
_____
_____

List the things that make you unique

_____ _____
_____ _____
_____ _____
_____ _____

What Categories do people try to put you in? What labels do they try to give you?

_____
_____

_____

_____

How are you going to break these stereotypes?

_____

_____

_____

_____

My Own Life Rule #4 _____

_____

Ps 139:14 I will praise You; for I am fearfully and wonderfully made; Your works are marvelous and my soul knows it very well.

Rule # 5

NEVER-EVER Leave Another Angel
Hanging. This is a Cardinal Sin!

If you have true friends, hold on to them. Do not leave them hanging in a time of need. Be a true friend too - do not lie, speak truth, be real, have fun, but know your limits. Do not compromise **you** for others! That is FAKE! And lastly, if you see your friend heading for a ditch, don't just watch! Jump your butt over there and grab them. If you save them –cool. If not you went down TOGETHER! That is an Angel!

True friends are very hard to come by. Everyone you meet is not your friend. Friends are people you can trust, count on, have things in common with, and they should have a personality you like. Trust, loyalty, and being reliable are all traits of a real friend and they are things you cannot measure over night. Don't call everyone your friend. Friendship takes time. It's risky business. You don't know you can trust someone until it comes up. A friend should be someone you don't have to think around. You can let your guard down. They should care for you and you for them. Friends keep your secret thoughts, desires, and dreams.

  An Angel would never tell the secrets of another Angel. We know that the key to friendship is listening and loving. If you're the one everyone tells all their "dirt" to, don't betray them. If you have to get it out or release it – write it down in a "secrets" book. Let your mom or sibling be your go to person – someone you can trust. DO NOT TELL YOUR BOYFRIEND EVERYTHING THAT IS GOING ON WITH YOUR FRIENDS. Boys gossip. He will repeat it and if it gets too bad, he will question your actions and character because you hang around those people. Furthermore, if they have that much drama you might want to check that yourself! Don't say something about people that you would not say to them face to face. This is hard, but it will keep you out of a lot of mess. When people are discussing others around me, I may listen. If I decide to say something, I ask myself, "Am I prepared to repeat this?" If the answer is no, I just keep it to myself. I live by my own rules. I have to be true to who I am, which leads me to the next part of this rule; be yourself!

Many teenage girls try to force themselves into groups to be popular. An Angel is always true to who she is. We do not bend our principles, personalities, or character so that we can hang out with certain people. I have learned that people want to hang out with me because I am myself. If you stay true to who God made you, you actually give other girls the freedom to stop "faking the funk" and to be themselves also. If you have to pretend you like a certain thing to be in a group, – DON'T. If you have to hold your tongue about things you feel very strong about to be friends with someone – THAT PERSON IS NOT YOUR FRIEND!

Friends respect your opinion, even if it's not their own. My best friend and I are very much alike, but there are some very BIG differences. I'm black, she's white. She seems mean, I am mean! Well, not really, I call it direct. I am conservative but she is ultra conservative in some areas and very liberal in others. I don't hold her views in those areas, but because I respect her as a person – I respect our differences. When those things come up – we know where each other stand. I'm not going to pretend to agree with her so we can be friends. We are friends in spite of our differences. I need to say one thing, while Shauna and I have differences the things we have in common are what holds us together – we are both devoted Christians, we had the same upbringing, we both are social studies teachers, we both have coached cheerleading, dance, directed pageants so on and so on. My point is you should have some obvious connections to your friends. People will assume you are like your friends, so you need to hang out with people that have your character and values.

I remember when I was a junior in high school I met this group of guys that were in a dance group, as I was. I really liked one of them. He was so charming and attractive; ok, he was "hot"! Whenever he looked at me, I knew he was checking me out. He called me every once in a while. He would hang close by when we all went out together. He even made a four-hour trip to visit me during my freshmen year at college. But he never asked me out. During our sophomore year of college, we all got together again. I got his number and confessed my feelings. He told me something that changed my perspective on friendship forever. I had a friend that lied a lot and kept up mess in the group. There was always drama surrounding her, and I hated it, but I loved her. He told me that he really hated her! He said, "I watched you, liked you, wanted to talk to you. You seemed so nice, funny and cute, of course. But I kept telling myself if she is always hanging with "her" for all this time, she has to be like her. So I just counted you as a friend, 'cause I didn't want that type of drama in my life."

I was crushed; and yes, tears fell. All I could think was how I had let someone else get in the way of my desires. But most importantly, I was so hurt to know that this guy that I held in high esteem, thought of me in that way. WOW! What else had my "friends" kept me from? I had grown up with this person, so I felt obligated to keep her as a friend. But in that moment, I learned that sometimes in order to grow, you have to let go of some things or people. It wasn't too long after this that I distanced myself from her and after a few nasty words slung my way and rumors later - I got over it and moved on. If you look at your friends, what will their behaviors (actions and values) say about you? Remember this borrowed phrase - "Show me your friends and I'll show you your future." Pastor Benjamin Lang, Cornerstone Baptist Church, Lithia Springs, Ga.

There is one thing you should know about friendship: everyone you meet is not "for" you. What does "for you" mean? Let's use Jeans for an example. You and a girlfriend may wear the same size; but when you go to the mall and try on the same pair of jeans, she may look great in them but you don't. Do you buy them anyway? No, you keep looking until you find something that fits your figure. YOU want the best fit! Now you both look great at the skating rink. It's the same with people. Being your **best** is the most important gift you can give your friends.

Everyone you meet is not going to be around when you are 40; some may not even be around next month. That's okay. There are going to be people who do not care for your personality or do not have the same interests as you, or the same style, or dreams. That's all okay. Some people come and go; and when they go, LET THEM! You are not a failure, a reject, bad, ugly, or wrong. Nor are you doomed to be alone if some people choose not to be in your life. It doesn't mean something is wrong with you. It means that a particular person was never meant to be a part of the full scope of your life. Let the imposter go with your blessings and be ready to receive genuine friendship from those that God places in your life.

Do not spin your wheels trying to keep people in your life. An Angel never tries to "make" people like her. I call this holding people hostage. If you have to be deceptive, jump through hoops, spend money, or settle with being the only one giving of themselves to be in any type of relationship, THAT RELATIONSHIP IS NOT FOR YOU!

Listen to Tyler Perry's take on relationships and how people fit into your life:

"Some people come into your life for a lifetime; some come for a season. You got to know which is which. You're gonna always mess up when you mix them seasonal people up with lifetime expectations. We got people that got married with people they only supposed to be with for a season, and they wonder why they have so much hell in their life. That was a person that was supposed to come and teach you one thing. You didn't know it so you just fell in love, and now you wonder why don't got no peace anywhere you go.

I put everybody that comes in my life in the category of a tree. Some people are like leaves on a tree. The wind blows; they over there. They [are] unstable. Wind blows the other way; they over here. Seasons change; they wither and die. [They are] gone. That's alright. Most people in the world are like that. They just there to take from the tree. They [are] there to take and give shade every now and then. That's all they can do. But don't get mad at ['em]; that's who they are. Some people are like a branch on that tree. You gotta be careful with them branches too cause they'll fool you. They'll get there and make you think they a good friend and real strong, but the minute you step out there on ['em,] they'll break and leave you high and dry. But if you find you two or three people in your life that's like the roots at the bottom of the tree, you are blessed. They're the kind of people that ain't goin' nowhere. They ain't worried about bein' seen, don't nobody have to know that they know you, they ain't got to know what they doin' for you. But if them roots wasn't there that tree couldn't live. You understand? When you get you some roots, hold on to em'. But the rest of it you let it go. Just let folks go."

Madea from "Madea goes to Jail".

The last thing an AIT should consider about friendships is this: when you find people that want to be a part of your life, help with your visions, support your dreams and will be honest with you about whatever – LET THEM!!!!!!

We need to stop the insanity of being with people that look a certain way, have certain things or can get us this or that. Please know all that comes with a price. Shall we go back to Count the Cost!?

Genuine, true friends are hard to come by and some of us miss out because we are trying to run in behind the wrong people. I speak of what I know. In all my sulking over lost friendships I thought about the people I "dissed" to be with the wrong people. What a waste! Don't make the same mistakes! When everything else fails, be what you are looking for. Be what God has destined you to be!

My Rule 5 Thoughts

_____
_____
_____
_____
_____
_____
_____
_____
_____
_____
_____
_____
_____
_____
_____
_____
_____
_____
_____
_____
_____
_____
_____
_____
_____

List your closest friends

_____ _____

_____ _____

_____ _____

_____ _____

Who do you really trust from your list?

_____

_____

_____

_____

What are the characteristics of a good friend?

_____

_____

_____

_____

_____

Do YOU have these characteristics?   Yes / No
Which ones do you need to work on?

_____

_____

_____

My own life Rules #5_____

_____

Pr 18:24 ¶ A man that hath friends must shew himself friendly: and there is a friend that sticketh closer than a brother.

Friendship Pages

Place pictures and notes about friends here

Friendship Pages

Place pictures and notes about friends here

Rule # 6

"It Is What It Is," means "It Is What YOU Make It."

While we cannot control the things that happen to and around us, our reaction to those things plays a huge part in how they affect us. An Angel must always use wisdom before she responds to uncontrollable events. You can't stop friends from walking away or people from making up stuff to say. You can't control your parents' mood swings or if they fight a lot. If your dad or mom doesn't visit frequently or your teachers just don't understand, your grandmother can't afford the latest Jordan's or whatever shoe is out now, none of this is your fault. Stop accepting the blame for things you cannot manage or control, especially for conditions that involve you.

When you are facing these types of obstacles, you have to think before you act. Ask yourself, "What can I control in this situation?" Most likely the answer will be, "My reaction." Flying off the handle because Latoya was talking about you in third period is the reason you got detention, not Latoya's big mouth. I know your natural reaction may be to retaliate, or lash out to save face, but all those thoughtless efforts are going to get you is more drama, trouble, or bigger problems. If your mom is all moody and snapping at you, do you really think slamming doors or yelling back is going to help you out? In my house it will get you put out! So let's use wisdom and think before we act.

You don't know what to do or say? You aren't sure how to react? The first thing you need to know is God never wanted you to handle life's trials and tribulations alone. I know many teens think they are invincible, but take it from someone who learned the hard way; His way is better.

I'm reminded of the hymn "What a friend We Have in Jesus" While this song is not as catchy as something by Kirk Franklin, Beyonce', or Mary Mary, it's old fashioned language teaches a timeless lesson that transcends all ages :

What a Friend we have in Jesus, all our sins and griefs to bear!
What a privilege to carry everything to God in prayer!
O what peace we often forfeit, O what needless pain we bear,
All because we do not carry everything to God in prayer.
Have we trials and temptations? Is there trouble anywhere?
We should never be discouraged; take it to the Lord in prayer.
Can we find a friend so faithful who will all our sorrows share?
Jesus knows our every weakness; take it to the Lord in prayer.
Are we weak and heavy laden, cumbered with a load of care?
Precious Savior, still our refuge, take it to the Lord in prayer.
Do your friends despise, forsake you? Take it to the Lord in prayer!
In His arms He'll take and shield you; you will find a solace there.
Blessed Savior, Thou hast promised Thou wilt all our burdens bear.
May we ever, Lord, be bringing all to Thee in earnest prayer.
Soon in glory bright unclouded there will be no need for prayer
Rapture, praise and endless worship will be our sweet portion there.

Looking at the words of this 154 year old hymn, we can learn a lot. The hymn tells us that Christ bears our sins and griefs- heartaches, misery, and pain. The word "bear" means to endure, to put up with, to suffer, to stand in the gap for, to shoulder, carry, or take on. So Jesus took on your sin and my sin. If you have accepted

Him and if you allow Him, He will endure your pains, sorrows, and griefs (heartaches).

But the problem is we don't talk to God about our problems. We don't trust Him. We are a generation that does not KNOW Him! We have no idea how God can truly handle our situations because we never give Him the chance. But how can you ever learn to trust Him if you never try Him? Don't you try on shoes before you buy them? We taste things to decide if we like it or not. We try on a pair of jeans. We ask for a sample at the buffet before we order. But we decide that God isn't real or doesn't care about us before we ever talk to Him! Christ wants to be a part of your every day life. He wants to "share your sorrows." But the key is to, say it with me, **Take it to the LORD in prayer**. Prayer will help relieve the stress of your situation and talking to God about your issues is a great way to deal with people you cannot control – remember God can! An Angel understands who is really in control, and we keep a very close connection to Him.

Use Wisdom when reacting to your situations:
Some people are born with great wisdom but others receive it as a result of prayer. Need to know what wisdom is? My pastor gives an excellent explanation so I see no need to change it: Wisdom is doing the **Right**

Thing, at the **Right Time**, for the **Right Reasons**, to get the **Right Result**. When you are about to react to a situation ask yourself – is your response going to produce the outcome you want? If so, "Do you, Boo!" If not, you need to rethink your plan.

It really bothers me when people shrug off their bad behavior and the consequences like it just fell on them out of the sky. When you say, "It is what it is," you are saying that you give up. You're really saying that you relinquish all responsibility for your own actions. You can't hide your head in the sand. You don't get off so easily. *"Be not deceived; God is not mocked: for whatsoever a man soweth, that shall he also reap."* (Galatians 6:7)

There are a couple of principles you must understand. You put things in motion in your life with your own words and your actions. Like Newton's Laws of Motion, every action has an equal reaction. If you gossip, you will get gossip. If you think negatively, you will get negative. If you are plotting against your enemy, please believe your own demise is coming. There is a biblical principal that says, "You shall have what you say." Mark 11:23 Remember that The Almighty Himself created us with His words and His Desire. So in the same vein, place your words carefully and your actions even more so. Think about this; people speak things on themselves and others every day. We say, "I'm not going to make it," or "you will amount to nothing." We are constantly placing thoughts into the atmosphere and then are surprised when they come back to us.

Think of the law of motion as mans attempt to understand God's ways. IT is a natural way to explain a spiritual principle. Every action has an equal and opposite reaction.

Let's look at it: Whenever a first body exerts a force **F** on a second body, the second body exerts a force −**F** on the first body. **F** and −**F** are equal in size and opposite in direction.

So when you place your words into the atmosphere, the force of your words will cause a force to be excreted back in your direction, and that force DEPENDS on the frequency used. In other words, if you keep saying something, it is going to build up and come back with that same level of force.
I know some may not understand this yet, but I think it is extremely important to get it in your spirit for the day you do.

YOU have the power to make something great or not so great out of your life. The decisions that you make, the things you do, and the words you say will determine how far you go in life. So, when things happen, and you know you put it ALL in motion; don't look around like "I don't know what happened!" Especially around other Angels because Rule # 5 dictates that we tell you!

My Rule 6 Thoughts

_____

_____

_____

_____

_____

_____

_____

_____

_____

_____

_____

_____

_____

_____

_____

_____

_____

_____

_____

_____

_____

_____

_____

_____

_____

Watch your words

Things you need to stop saying about yourself;

_____

_____

_____

_____

_____

_____

What does God say about you?   (Ps.139:14)

_____

_____

_____

_____

_____

Name someone you recently had an argument with

_____

_____

_____

How did you react to the situation?

_____

_____

_____

_____

My Life Rule #6_____

_____

Mark 11:24 Therefore I say unto you, What things soever ye desire, when ye pray, believe that ye receive them, and ye shall have them. Jas 1:19 Wherefore, my beloved brethren, let every man be swift to hear, slow to speak, slow to wrath:

Rule # 7

Don't Ask an Angel a Question If You Don't Want The Real Answer.

If you are looking for someone to "puff you up" or lie to you, don't ask an Angel her opinion or what she thinks about your situation or decisions. Remember: Angels are bound to the other rules when they answer. So if your outfit is NOT HOT, someone is going to tell you. If you are going in the wrong direction or the NEW GUY just isn't the RIGHT GUY, **WE ARE GOING TO CALL IT LIKE IT IS!!!**

We are not afraid of being real with you. We are not afraid of upsetting you because we were so direct. Hey, that's why you asked one of us the question in the first place!! While we may seem extremely frank or blunt to you, know that it is for your good. We are that way with each other. Remember truth breeds trust. Isn't that what you are looking for?

Now that I've said all that, let's get one thing clear. An Angel would never correct, dishonor, or "call out" another Angel in public. We have these types of very real conversations in an intimate, secure, private, and safe environment. I would hope that my friends would never tell me not to wear my new red dress again because it makes me look dumpy at the Social Studies Department's lunch table while everyone else is listening. If my fly is down, my skirt caught in my tights, or something is exposed, pull me to the side and tell me immediately. True friends NEVER embarrass those they love.

I am very frank with my friends because I want what is best for them. I am open to their honest opinions about things in my life. If you can't trust the words of those around you, you need new friends!

One of the areas an AIT must grow in is true inner confidence. If you are asking too many questions and relying on the opinions of others too much, someone is going to start questioning you!!!!

Great leaders are not right all the time, but they do know how to make a decision and stick to it. When things are going wrong they know how to recognize that fact and make adjustments. People do not trust leadership because of a 100% track record. They follow others because they have confidence in their ability to work it out along the way. An Angel is a leader in that she can make a decision and knows how to surround herself with confident and competent people to help WHEN she does need council. REMEMBER THAT!

Angel Tip: Being "real" doesn't give you the license to be rude. Do not use this rule as a permit for just telling people what you think about them, or to "read" them. If that's what you are getting from this, you are completely missing the point. You "<u>earn</u>" the right to speak into people's lives.

I remember the first couple of "Real" conversations Shauna and I had. We had been friends for about three years, and were clearly interested in the best for each other. After sharing real issues and secret thoughts about different situations we were in, it was natural to have feelings and opinions about those things. For about four months our conversations were started with what is now a signature phrase between us, "How close of friends are we...." The response... "We're close, Why?"

Then one of us would share something we only write about or keep deep within, or we would expound on our thoughts over what the other told us a couple of conversations earlier. We were VERY careful not to betray that trust, nor to over step bounds until the other was ready. This is what I mean by "earning the right to speak."

I will forever remember another relationship that never stood a chance because I spoke to a situation before the other person was ready and open to my "Angel-realness." My lack of understanding about timing and gauging another's willingness to be transparent severed an opportunity to develop a friendship or at least probably a connection. I failed to "Know my Audience..."

You need trustworthy people that will speak truth into your life and at the same time you need to actively develop your own decision making skills. An Angel NEVER uses her insight and boldness to humiliate, cut, or emotionally assassinate others. We speak life! That's an Angel!

My Rule 7 Thoughts

1 Jo 2:5 But whoso keepeth his word, in him verily is the love of God perfected: hereby know we that we are in him.

How do you respond to the criticisms of others?

Who can tell you "like it is" without offending you?

Are you confident in your decisions? _____

What are some areas you need to make better
decisions? _____

_____

_____

Do you need to trust yourself more or take more time
to think things through? _____

Whose opinion do you trust?

Someone once told me, "Show me your friends and I'll
show you your future." Do the people you surround
yourself with truly have your best interest at heart?
Would they tell you that skipping Algebra to hang out

with a couple of football players is a really bad decision or would they just go along with you?

What kind of friend are you?

Would you tell your friend if they were about to make a bad decision or go down the wrong path?

_____

_____

_____

Are there some things you need to share with your friend but have not? If so explain why..._____

_____

_____

_____

Can you be trusted?

My Rule 7 of Life_____

_____

Hebrews 4:12 For the word of God is quick, and powerful, and sharper than any two-edged sword, piercing even to the dividing asunder of soul and spirit, and of the joints and marrow, and is a discerner of the thoughts and intents of the heart.

Rule# 8

An Angel Cannot Be Out Done.

Angels are always busy with this project or that.
When they put their hands to it, something wonderful
is bound to happen. Angels are the "go to" person in a
group. What this phrase means is "Give it to an Angel;
she'll do it right." They're the ones you want behind the
scenes when polish is needed for your desired result!
They put serious thought into every detail of every
endeavor. It is because of their very personality that
Rule #1 came to be.

Angelesque girls want to make every event the "bestest,
most slpentiferic, spectaculariousies" thing ever (in the
words of Tigger of course!). They always want things
to be perfect. This can be a down fall because things
aren't always perfect and Angels have a hard time
embracing this concept. An Angel Project is hard to top.
They naturally think over the top. So, they make the

average "non- Angel's" attempt a boring effort at best! When you begin a project, whether it's in History class, Student government elections, a bake sale for French Club, Homecoming, or redecorating your room, you should give it your very best effort. Half doing things can leave you with an incomplete feeling. You want to be able to look at your accomplishments with pride and satisfaction. This goes for home projects, homework, and even your high school experience. As an Angel you do not want to just "exist" during high school. You want to experience it. Use your gifts and talents to make your teen years a time to remember not a time of regrets.

As you attempt the impossible and start laying a foundation for your dreams, take lots of pictures, write down your feelings, and share your good and bad times with people that care about you. Angels put their all into the things they do. We love taking on projects for people about whom we care. Remember, the greatest expression of love is your time. So, our hard work is an attempt to put our love and care into some tangible form. It's our love, our heart, our core that we are pouring out for others and ourselves. You can't top that!

With that said this is a good place to revisit your attention to finding your purpose. Remember that the

Earth is better just by your presence. God sent you here on assignment and it is your Angelistic responsibility to find out what that is and to pour "you" out into the atmosphere. As you affect the world with your talents and gifts, know that no one can "do you" like you can and once you have a clear and genuine connection back to your creator, the LORD through Jesus Christ, your efforts to be the "You" you were called to be can NEVER be out done!

Let me encourage you to fight to be the person God called you to be. Don't let friends or foes, poverty nor riches, fads or fades divert you from this one thing. If someone is telling you, you can't, speak **"I Can!"** If someone is telling you, you won't, speak louder, **"I Will!"** If you are in a situation where money or family are the hindering spirit you are going to have to find the resolve to "Be" in spite of your surroundings. You can do it. You're an Angel!

An Angel's Daily Prayer:

LORD, help me to be all You have ordained me to be. Give me the wisdom to walk in the right path and the vision to see myself the way You see me. Give me Divine connections with those you have preordained to speak into my life. Give me favor in those areas you have ordered for me to go. LORD, I speak divine wisdom and understanding over myself as I prepare for my purpose. Protect me from the things of this world; from the drugs and crime and the spirit of depression and fear. Cover me as I grow and keep my mind as the ills of life try to change who you called me to be. Let my mind be open to the things of God and to the concepts and skills I will glean from teachers and instructors as I get ready to affect this world for Your purposes and Kingdom. Show me Your ways. *Teach me Oh LORD the ways of thy statutes and I will keep them till the end. Just give me understanding and I will keep thy laws. I will observe them with my whole heart.*

My Rule 8 Thoughts

Ro 8:31 What shall we then say to these things? If God be for us, who can be against us?

List the projects you are currently engaged in

What are some things you want to do?

Do you really give things your best effort? Y / N
If not, how can you put more into the things that you do?

Things You Need for a Great Angel Project

1. Camera
2. Planner
3. Notebook for notes, sketches , and materials lists
4. Time Line
5. To Do List
6. A Who Does What List – if it is a group project

Pray the Angel Prayer Regularly.

Having favor in high places is always a sure fire way to ensure great results!

My Rule 8 of Life _____

_____

_____

Philippians 4:13 I can do all things through Christ which strengtheneth me.

Rule # 9

Do Not Call Your Self an Angel When You're Not.

We could say it like this....An Angel NEVER pretends to be something she's not! But the shock value of the prior statement is so Angelesque!

Everyone has their own specialty, their own personality, attitudes, and character. We all have our own special purpose. An endearing old friend taught me that every person has a specific purpose in the Earth – an assignment given to you directly by God to carry out in this Earth. That makes each of us special, important, and valued. Knowing this makes it insulting when we try to "reinvent" ourselves to fit into a group or crowd. You need to embrace who you are. Don't force yourself into social groups for popularity's sake. This is in violation of Rule # 5.

Angels aren't groupies.

They don't "need" to be a part of any sect, club, or "social group." While some of us choose to be affiliated with various community groups, we can stand alone, and when my beliefs are in question, I will stand all by myself if I have to! You would never catch a true Angel as a member of a gang or dealing in criminal activity. We see such affiliations as harmful not only to our dreams, but the dreams of others. Those groups are fatuitous (dumb), a waste of time, and counterproductive to everything we believe in.

Each member of the Angels is an Angel all by herself.

This simply means you have to be a whole person. You hear girls and women say things like, "Oh he completes me," or "My better half," or "I'm incomplete without 'them'." These are phrases that indicate WRONG THINKING! Girls that follow the Angel philosophy understand that we don't need each other to make us whole, we CHOOSE each other to make us rounded!

Everybody needs people in their lives and if you try to live in isolation you will never experience the richness of all the things life has to offer you. An Angel knows that adding other Angelesque girls to her own bubbly life will make for great fun and an explosion of awesome adventures and memories.

Knowing all that doesn't change who I am. My presence in the lives of other Angels doesn't make them who they are, and even though I love goofing off with them, they do not make me who I am. I am me because God made me, not my friends. God spoke into me and breathed this goofiness into my heart – NOT MAN! An Angel has to be able to stand their ground, you can't be easily swayed, and you should not allow others to push you around. Be prepared to go against the grain when your upbringing is put to the test. Matter of fact, our ability to stand alone is a major quality that makes one an Angel.

You show me a talented, gifted, spunky young lady who thinks for herself, has her own things going, and is really too busy living to notice what I'm doing – and I'll show you a true Angel. The concept behind Angels is the idea of gathering these single whole units to complete a task together – it usually is quite a site. Everyone brings something to the table. We are task oriented. WE LIKE Challenging THINGS! There are no tag-a-longs here! If being an Angel is not your thing that is so ok. There is a place for you. You just have to press into God so you can find it. Find your spot and get in it...I can't share mine.

The things your parents and loved ones have taught you are very important in the make-up of your foundation. There is a concept called spiritual gifts and a lot of times you can see the attributes of talent flow through the generations of a family. Or, you can look at your family and see similar talents in them. This is why it is so important for young people to know their family history and a little about their ancestry. Your teen years are not the time to pull away and put down everything you know about your family. It is the time to take that knowledge and all you have observed, branch out, and place your own stake into the soil of your family foundation. Who are you? Look to your past to see what you can pull from, then search within to decide what you have to help you move forward.

What if you don't have parents to guide and inspire you? What If your examples are not good ones? So many of us have had to deal with these facts. We have missing pieces of our lives so we really aren't sure what we are! Let's look at this a while.

Let's say your parents aren't the best examples to follow. Maybe your dad dealt in drugs, hustled, or was

involved in some type of criminal activity. Maybe your
mother used people or drugs, stole, or did things that
weren't ethical. How do you look at that as an example
of your spiritual gifts?

First, you understand that all people are given some
level of gifting by God to contribute to the world.
Secondly, you understand that people don't always use
those gifts and talents to glorify God and uplift the
Kingdom. Thirdly, I want you to tell yourself that
their path **DOES NOT** have to be yours. Next, we realize
that people do abuse and squander the gifts given to
them. The last thing I want to show you will take a
little concentration, go with me.

Think about the things you watched your parents do.
What did they spend most of their time doing? Now
don't look at the action. Ask yourself a question. What
skill did they need, use, and do well to do those things?
If your dad was constantly hustling people, was he good
at it? Stay with me; I mean was he good at talking to
people? Did they believe in the things he said? Did
people follow him? Did he keep people's attention? As
horrible as criminal activity is, and as badly as it hurts
others, teachers, social workers and school counselors
can identify the positive talents and skills embedded in
criminal activity. If you ask, an educator can tell you

the legitimate and legal occupations the person COULD have done well. So I want you to see them like I would if I were their teacher

- A drug dealer has to know math, chemistry and PR (Public Relations)
- Hustlers have to be able to talk with knowledge of the topic and sound like they have a particular education in a subject. They have to know a little about business because they have to produce a product.
- Thieves are great "readers" of character and are very aware of their surroundings
- Women that use people are great actresses and judges of character. Think about it; all these people know who to "try" and who not to.

Now I'm not glorifying any of this mess. Delete that thought! I am really trying to help someone. If you are caught up in these life-ending, dead-end activities because you think you don't have anything to offer the world – We just covered at least 10 different skills that can earn six figures if you just focus your efforts in the right direction. The same skills that one uses for immoral gain, another can use to benefit the world.

What if you don't have any positive examples in a parent? How do you see your generational trends, talents, and gifts? I have a couple of suggestions;

1. **ASK** – you have the right to know where you come from, and who you come from. There is something freeing and empowering in having an ancestral history. Take a deep breath and ask some questions. Your family may be reluctant to talk to you because the topic brings them pain. Show your family members that you are not judging them. Let them know that having an understanding of your background will help you map out your future and to understand yourself. If one won't talk to you go to another – be relentless...it's your future!

2. **Look within** – God has given you everything you need to be the greatest "You" ever. Spend some time looking at your likes and dislikes. How do you learn best? What would you rather spend your time doing? What is the one thing you would do for the rest of your life – FOR FREE! That is your area of talent and possibly your purpose. Start by taking the learning styles test in the appendix. Then learn about your personality by taking a Myers Briggs test. *An online testing address is included in the*

appendix. Then take a questionnaire that will tell you the occupations that go with your talents and interest.

3. **Allow God to be your guide**. If you feel your life is bad because you don't have the parents that others have, I dare you to put God to the test in this area. God has everything you need to be all that you need to be. Christ died so you would have a direct connection with the Father of all. God wants to be your parent.

I was about 9 when I decided to follow Christ, and I spent my teen years learning just "what" and "who" God is. Through my years I found that In Him there is Provision; in Him there is safety; in Him there is Direction. In Christ I found deliverance from low-self esteem, rejection from friends and failed relationships, and lack of a relationship with my own father. My relationship with Christ helped me reach out and repair that non-relationship with my dad. In Christ I found the strength and courage to be myself and to reach for dreams that I know He placed inside me, when I was afraid of people and their thoughts of me. I found affirmation (encouragement and adoption) in Christ when people around me told me I would be nothing or tried to say what I COULD NOT do. Instead, God told me – You can DO ALL THINGS IN ME!

I spent three years of my life in seclusion; complete isolation, alone, all by myself. There were no phone calls, no friends, no going out, and no boy friends; only, my daughter and me. Then God began healing all the hurtful words spoken over me and building me up and teaching me that I am the Daughter of the Most High God.

Years later and many lessons learned, I have the best friend anyone could ask for – true, honest, loyal and she brings a lot to my life. I have the greatest husband – supportive, honest, true, loyal, "my rottweiler" (my students call him "Big Swoll"), intelligent, creative but most importantly – a man of principle and respecter of the character of God! I am NEVER alone because I have so many people around me now; former students, students, mentees, my own 5 kids, and now I have you! I never complain about being alone anymore. Reading about my experiences gives you a chance to believe that you too can be EVERYTHING you are supposed to be. And it's free, girl. You can't beat that!

I've found love, provision, direction, healing, and joy because of my relationship with Jesus Christ. If the people around you aren't cutting the mustard, why not try the one who made you? I'm just sayn'; My God is an excellent choice!

My Rule 9 Thoughts

_____

_____

_____

_____

_____

_____

_____

_____

_____

_____

_____

_____

_____

_____

_____

_____

_____

_____

_____

_____

_____

_____

_____

_____

_____

What does your name mean? Where does it come
from?_____

_____

_____

_____

What are your talents? (A specialty, often athletic, creative,
or artistic aptitude; the natural endowments of a person)

_____

_____

_____

_____

_____

What are your gifts? (To endow with some power, quality, or
attribute)

_____

_____

_____

_____

_____

_____

Map the Character/Talents/Gifts/Vocations of Your Family

Mother   Father

Grandmother   Grandmother

Grandfather   Grandfather

What is the one thing you would do every day for free?

_____

_____

My Life Rule #9 _____

_____

John 4:29 Come, see a man, which told me all things that ever I did: is not this the Christ?

Angel Rule # 10

Live The Life You Are Given!

This is so self explanatory. After you have applied all the Rules, and have dotted all your "i's" and crossed all your "t's," just live the hand you are dealt. As a matter a fact, you should apply this rule first!!!

The Rules are my way of remembering to be all God has called me to be. When fear sets in, I say to myself, "there's no such thing as over the top." When people around me try to bring me down or don't get my vision and I start to question myself, I remember "Do not allow others to affect me!" If I have more ideas than I have money, Rule #2 kicks in and I pull out my calendar and my planning skills kick in. Because my past issues were mainly relational, I have to keep that in mind. I recognize that every person that I meet is not for me, so I am able to see the greatness in others and still remember my place in God's grand plan – I don't have time for jealousy, envy or resentment about what others have, are, or accomplish. I actually use that to push myself - if they can, I can too! If I can, YOU CAN TOO!

God has gifted you with certain skills and talents. Use them to the best of your ability. See the greatness within. Be yourself. But, please don't try to be something you are not! If you invent a personality or create a character, you will spend the rest of your life's energy trying to keep up that facade and Angels like us can see right though it. Think about this. If people are going to talk about you, and they are, let it be true; let it be about how you are busting your butt to make things happen in and around your school and community. Whatever it is that you want to do - DO IT!

Don't stick your head in the sand and hide. Stop making excuses; do not wait to do it tomorrow - WHATEVER IT IS YOU WANT TO DO - DO IT!!!!! If it makes sense, if it has been your dream since you were a little tike, if you have visions about whatever it is every time you close your eyes, YOU"VE GOT TO REACH FOR IT!

LIVE BABY LIVE

Let's get one thing straight. I do not care that you are only 14 or 18. You don't have a life time to fumble through life trying to figure things out. Unplanned events are called mistakes, and mistakes have consequences. Angel 2, Shauna, would say that life is all about choices and sometimes you are going to mess it up. She's right of course; none of us are perfect. I just want you to be equipped to live the best life possible and as prepared as possible. You do not have time to waste in this life. Let me be the one between the two of us that has regrets, not you. You can use my life as your testimony and get it right now! If you mess up trying to be all you can be - that's alright with me! Rule 8 in full effect.

If you're with someone that does not appreciate your true value - dump them. If you think you have to sleep with a guy to keep him - kick yourself and then dump him!

If the girls you hang with are skipping class, smoking and drugging, or doing things to shorten their lives - drop them!

If you're lying to make yourself feel more important, stop it! If you are "dogging" the people around you to make yourself look better – it's not working so cut-it-out!

If you don't like the clothes you wear, your hair, the people you hang with, the direction you're going in, if you are doing a bunch of stuff just to say you are busy...

STOP THE INSANITY!!!!

Don't settle for whatever; be Who-"ever" God intended you to be. Be great, be good, live strong and laugh loud. Change lives, leave a trail, teach others, make your mark in this Earth – but make sure you have something worth following! LEARN....and then LIVE PEOPLE LIVE!

My Rule 1 0 Thoughts

_____
_____
_____
_____
_____
_____
_____
_____
_____
_____
_____
_____
_____
_____
_____
_____
_____
_____
_____
_____
_____
_____

The Angel Life Rules # 10 ~ Never changes....

The Angel Creed

Say it with me aloud;

I Will....

be courageous

be confident

hold my head up when I'm scared

Take two steps forward when I want to run away

Glide across the floor when I want to hide

Take a deep breath when I want to scream

Strut my stuff when I get it right

Jump back in when I mess it up

Smile when I want to yell

Cry when I want to cry

Love 'cause I need to love

Give myself a second chance

Give the world a third and fourth

Give the spirit of hate none at all

See People the way God sees them

Use my skills to change the world

Know that I am wonderfully made

Know that my life has great value.

I'm an Angel here on assignment

I will not leave until my work is done.

Your Angel Charge

If you can embrace the Angel Rules, Creed, and Biblical Principles that they represent, then you are ready to move from ATI status to being a real Angel!

Be sure to record your Angel Journey, and take lots of pictures...Lol

I'm Angel 1 and THIS has been another Angels' Production!

Appendix 1

1. "Youth AIDS – For Students" Population Services International.com2009

2. Dillon, Sam, "Large Urban-Suburban Gap Seen in Graduation Rates". pg. 14 New York Times April 22, 2009

3. Dean, Bob and Diamond, Laura "Report: Half of Atlanta students don't graduate on time." The Atlanta Journal Constitution April 1, 2008.

4. Holzman, M."Public Education & Black Male Students: The 2006 State Report Card." Schott Educational Inequity Index, Cambridge, MA; The Schott Foundation for Public Education. 2006

Appendix 2
Getting to Know Yourself

Most High school counselors are very knowledgeable about taking official IQ, Creativity or Career related tests. You can also find many of them on line. Some of the following web sites have free tests. Some have a minimum cost. Angels invest in their future. Take the test and buy shoes later!

Personality Test and Career Tests - Websites

1. www.lifescript.com/Search.aspx?q=Which_Type_Of_Career_Fits_Your_Personality

2. www.lifescript.com/Quizzes/Personality/What_Color_Is_Your_Personality

3. www.livecareer.com

4. http://www.myersbriggsreports.com

5. http://www.wherecreativitygoestoschool.com/vancouver/left_right/rb_test.htm

Appendix 3 – Biblical References

All scriptures and scriptural references were used from the *Power Bible CD Program*.

Power Bible CD is Copyright 2003 by Online Publishing, Inc.
127 N. Matteson Street PO Box 21, Bronson, MI 49028
bible@mail.com

Tech support: 1-517-369-6035

Please see the online help for additional copyright information.

Power BibleCD is programmed by Brandon Staggs.

Appendix 4
Resources

The following resources are influential to living an Angelquese life

1. Holman Christian Standard Bible (HCSB), used by the Fellowship of Christian Athletes

2. Act like a Lady, Think like a Man - Steve Harvey Amistad (January 27, 2009)

3. Don't make a Black Woman Take Off Her Earrings – Madea's Uninhibited commentary on Love and Life Tyler Perry, Penguin Group (February 2007)

4. Deliverance from Demons and Diseases: Freedom from Incurable Disease and Persistent Problems, Eric Hill, SunHill Publishers (May 31, 2004)

5. Secrets of the Vine: Breaking Through to Abundance, Bruce Wilkinson, Multnomah; 1 edition (March 29, 2001)

6. All materials by Michelle McKinney Hammond - http://www.michellehammond.com/

7. The Diva Principle, Michelle McKinney Hammond, Harvest House Publishers / 2004

Appendix 5
My Angels...

Women that influence me in their Angelseque living

My Mother – Barbara C. Summerville

My sisters, Angee and Lori Ann Summerville

Miriam D. Dufer- author, poet, very strong women

Vickie Elliot – play write, director, vocalist

Shauna C. Wilson – one bold woman

Rev. Tracey N Fletcher - educator, Pastor, mentor,
original Angel # 1

MarryAnn Hudson – Rest in Peace my good friend

Lille Summerville and Bernice Chapple – my truest
examples of strength in a time of trouble

Elder Bernice King

The Late Coretta Scott King

Oprah Winfrey

Dorothy Dandridge

Ella Baker

And Women of the 40s – when we were colored...

About the Author

 Wendy Torres is the founder of Angel's Productions. Through Angel's Productions Wendy has been able to put many of her talents and gifts to work. Angel's Productions was birthed out of her desire to help equip all young people of every socioeconomic background for their future.

Wendy has been teaching in the public schools of Georgia for over 14 years, and gained her knowledge of proper planning through the production of educational programs in the areas of cultural diversity, black history, community service projects to Kenya, Africa, and New Delhi, India, Marching Band Dance Auxiliary Competitions, School and Regional Social Studies Fairs, Poetry and Literary Recitations, Step Team Expositions, and the development of school and personal mentoring programs.

In her love for music she has spent 21 years working with gospel Choirs and the last 20 years working with young people is some musical capacity, drama, vocal training, choir and choral music, competition, urban dance, and lyrical dance. She currently works with individuals as the prepare for college and scholarship auditions.

While her ministry is not limited to youth, God has truly blessed her with a special patience, insight, and testimony that speaks to the Purpose and Destiny and needs of this, "Remnant Generation" of teenagers. As a part of the Joshua Generation, Wendy possesses the spirit of perseverance and refuses to believe the spies report that this current generation is lost, hopeless, and without restoration quality.

"They are today's Remnant and in that there is great power, heart, strength, and boldness. With our inexhaustible prayer, love, truthful revelation of the Word of God and its relevance to this present time, They will possess the Promise Land and lead "us" into a new Era of Kingdom living. They will possess the Land!" Wendy R. Torres.

Learn more about The Angel Rules and the Angels at angelsproductions.org; Followers of The Angel Rules on Facebook; or follow Wendy Torres on Twitter – angel1wendy.